Martha Washington
LOYAL PUBLIC SERVANT

BY TYLER OMOTH

Published by The Child's World®
1980 Lookout Drive • Mankato, MN 56003-1705
800-599-READ • www.childsworld.com

Photographs ©: Georgios Art/iStockphoto, cover, 1; Everett Historical/Shutterstock
Images, 5; De Agostini Picture Library/De Agostini/Getty Images, 6; North Wind
Picture Archives, 9, 15; iStockphoto, 10, 12, 16; Universal History Archive/Universal
Images Group/Getty Images, 19; PhotoQuest/Archive Photos/Getty Images, 20

ISBN 9781503824003
LCCN 2017944741

Printed in the United States of America
PA02362

ABOUT THE AUTHOR

Tyler Omoth has written more than 30 books for kids, covering a wide variety
of topics. He has also published poetry and award-winning short stories.
He loves sports and new adventures. Tyler currently lives in sunny Brandon,
Florida, with his wife, Mary.

TABLE OF
CONTENTS

FAST FACTS

Full Name

- Martha Dandridge Custis Washington

Birthdate

- June 2, 1731, in New Kent County, Virginia

Husband

- President George Washington

Children

- Martha had four children by her first marriage to Daniel Parke Custis: Daniel, Frances, John, and Martha.

Years in White House

- 1789–1797

Accomplishments

- Martha is the only First Lady to have her picture on U.S. paper currency. Her image appeared on the $1 silver certificate in 1886.
- During the Revolutionary War (1775–1783), Martha helped raise money to aid the Continental Army.

Chapter 1

A WOMAN OF SUBSTANCE

Martha Washington held her hands clasped in front of her as she sat on the presidential **barge**. Her husband, George, was by her side as the boat made its way through the Upper Bay into New York. She had traveled from Mount Vernon, Virginia. It had been a long trip. At some cities, Martha was greeted with parades and the ringing of bells. She wasn't used to so much attention, but people were excited and wanted to celebrate. George was to be the young nation's first president. That meant that Martha would be the first First Lady of the United States.

◄ Martha Washington once confessed that she did not particularly enjoy being First Lady.

Martha thought back to simpler times when she was a child. She remembered the wind rushing through her hair as she rode horses through the green countryside of Virginia. She could almost feel the dirt between her fingers from her lessons in gardening. She thought of her father. He had insisted that Martha learn more than just sewing and running a household. Even as a child, she embraced the chance to learn reading, math, and writing. She knew that very few girls her age had such an opportunity.

"I am still determined to be cheerful and to be happy in whatever situation I may be."[1]

—Martha Washington

When Martha turned 18 years old, she married Daniel Parke Custis. They were married for seven years. He was a wealthy landowner. She had been happy running the Custis household, but Daniel passed away in 1757. Martha suddenly found herself in charge of the household, the **plantation**, and all that came with them.

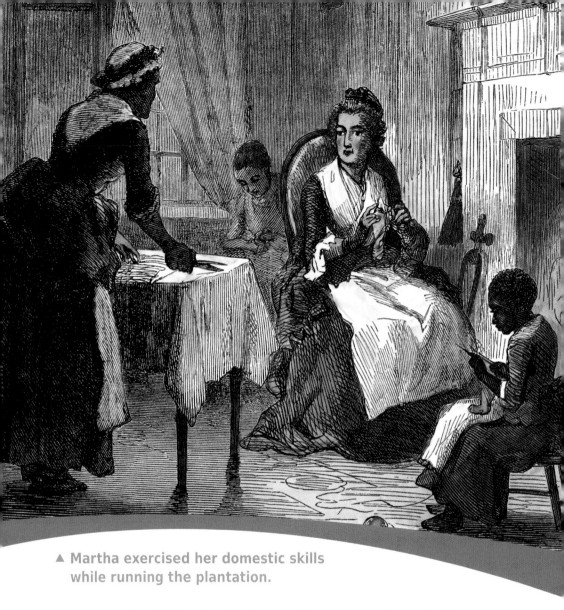

▲ Martha exercised her domestic skills while running the plantation.

Martha didn't back down. She remembered all she could from her education and took charge of the Custis plantation. Martha became a very successful woman. She owned 17,500 acres (7,080 ha) of productive cropland.

Chapter 2

MEETING GENERAL WASHINGTON

Martha took a deep breath to prepare herself as she entered the Williamsburg, Virginia, **ball**. Her husband, Daniel, had died just months before, but she needed to meet and talk with other people. Life at the plantation could be very lonely. When Martha entered the room, she immediately noticed a tall man surrounded by others. His name was George Washington. Soon, a mutual friend introduced them. Despite George being more than a foot taller than Martha, he looked her in the eye and spoke to her like an equal. She liked that. The pair developed a mutual affection for each other and decided to get married.

◄ George visited Martha and her children at the Custis plantation after Martha's husband died.

▲ Martha and George married on January 6, 1759.

Now Martha had two households to run. Her plantation was still operating, and George had a significant **estate** at Mount Vernon. George was a colonel, and he was frequently away from home. This left Martha in charge of managing both homes, but she was up to the task.

By 1774, Martha began to worry. The **colonies** were unhappy under British rule, and there was talk of a revolution. She thought of her husband and his successful military career. If there was a war, he was sure to play a **prominent** role in it. She turned out to be right. By 1775, the Revolutionary War had begun. George was made the head of the Continental Army. The soldiers in this army fought for America's independence from Britain.

"I had long since placed all the prospects of my future worldly happyness in the still enjoyments of the fireside at Mount Vernon."[2]

—*Martha Washington*

Another battle for life and death was sweeping across the countryside. Families fought to keep their children safe from a dangerous disease called **smallpox**. Martha decided to get herself and her children **inoculated** against the disease. It was a dangerous treatment, but it was their best chance to survive.

Martha also wanted to visit her husband's military camp. But no one was allowed near it who had not been inoculated.

Martha went to George's military camp as soon as she could. One general noted, "Mrs. Washington is excessive[ly] fond of the General and he of her. They are very happy in each other."[3] As Martha wandered through the military camp, she could see how difficult life was for the soldiers.

Martha entertained generals and their wives alongside her husband. She thought about ways to help the struggling soldiers. She realized that the biggest problem they faced was a lack of proper supplies. When she came home, Martha spoke to the public to raise money for the army. If her husband was going to lead them to victory, she would make sure they had the supplies they needed to get the job done.

Only two of Martha's children, John and Martha, survived ▶ past childhood.

Chapter 3

THE FIRST FIRST LADY

Martha handed the tray of tea to her servant and straightened her long, green dress. Now that she was First Lady, it was her responsibility to host to a wide variety of people. Local politicians and visitors from Europe were frequent guests at presidential gatherings. Martha double-checked the tea and refreshments. She made sure that the musicians were playing at a pleasant volume. Though the United States of America was a new country, she tried to imitate the elegance of European customs in her parties.

◀ Martha hosted many formal parties as First Lady.

As the nation's first First Lady, Martha didn't have any instructions on what was expected of her. She did her best to help her husband maintain a dignified appearance by minding his clothing. She also represented them well at formal parties. Martha didn't care for the capital city, New York. It was too busy and dirty. She longed for the fresh air of the countryside.

"I little thought when the war was finished, that any circumstances could possibl[y] have happened which would call the General into public life again."[4]

—Martha Washington

In 1790, the capital was moved to Philadelphia, Pennsylvania. Martha continued to host dinner parties and stand by George's side as he served as the first president. As George's second **term** in office neared its end, he told Martha that he was not going to take a third term. It was time to go home.

▲ Martha and George raised their grandchildren, Nelly and George Washington Parke Custis.

As Martha rode in the bouncing wagon back to Mount Vernon, she thought about what it meant to be First Lady.

She had tried to remain dignified and friendly. She strove to represent her country as well as her husband. Though she was glad to be headed home, Martha hoped that she had set a high standard for First Ladies in the years and decades to come.

THINK ABOUT IT

- Do you think Martha set a high standard for what First Ladies should do while their husbands are president? Support your answer.
- As a plantation owner, Martha relied on the work of enslaved people to keep it running. Slavery was legal at the time, but do you think it was okay for a plantation owner to use slaves to make a living?
- Martha noticed that troops in the Revolutionary War were unhappy and that they lacked supplies. How do you think a lack of supplies hurt the military?

◄ Martha and George continued to be respected by many people after they left the White House.

GLOSSARY

ball (BAWL): A ball is a formal gathering that features dancing. Martha met George at a ball.

barge (BARJ): A barge is a long boat with a flat bottom. It was easier for Martha to travel by barge than by horse and carriage.

colonies (KAH-luh-nees): Colonies are areas of land that have been settled by a group of people from a different country. The colonies fought for independence from the British.

estate (ess-TATE): An estate is a large area of land, including a house. George was proud of his large estate with wheat fields.

inoculated (in-OK-yuh-late-id): To be inoculated is to have been injected with a weakened form of a disease to help the body fight against it. The soldiers were inoculated against smallpox.

plantation (plan-TAY-shuhn): A plantation is a large farm that grows crops, such as cotton. Martha was in charge of the Custis plantation.

prominent (PROM-uh-nunt): Something that is prominent is very noticeable or important. President of the United States is a very prominent job.

smallpox (SMAWL-poks): Smallpox is a dangerous and contagious disease that causes blisters, rash, and a high fever. Many soldiers died of smallpox during the Revolutionary War.

term (TURM): A term is a specific, limited amount of time. George decided his second term as president would be his last.

SOURCE NOTES

1. "Letter, Martha Washington to Mercy Otis Warren, December 26, 1789." *Martha Washington.* Center for History and New Media, n.d. Web. 10 July 2017.

2. Ibid.

3. "Biography of Martha Washington." *Martha Washington.* Mount Vernon, 2017. Web. 10 July 2017.

4. "Letter, Martha Washington to Mercy Otis Warren, December 26, 1789." *Martha Washington.* Center for History and New Media, n.d. Web. 10 July 2017.

TO LEARN MORE

Books

Bailer, Darice. *George Washington*. Mankato, MN: The Child's World, 2017.

Krull, Kathleen. *A Kids' Guide to America's First Ladies*. New York, NY: HarperCollins, 2017.

Roberts, Cokie. *Founding Mothers: Remembering the Ladies*. New York, NY: HarperCollins, 2014.

Web Sites

Visit our Web site for links about Martha Washington:

childsworld.com/links

Note to Parents, Teachers, and Librarians: We routinely verify our Web links to make sure they are safe and active sites. So encourage your readers to check them out!

INDEX